# COLORS &
# NUMBERS

# LOUISE HAY

# COLORS & NUMBERS

## Your Personal Guide to Positive Vibrations in Daily Life

**HAY HOUSE LLC**
Carlsbad, California • New York City
London • Sydney • New Delhi

**Published in the United States by:** Hay House LLC: www.hayhouse
.com® • **Published in Australia by:** Hay House Australia Pty. Ltd.:
www.hayhouse.com.au • **Published in the United Kingdom by:** Hay
House UK, Ltd.: www.hayhouse.co.uk • **Published in India by:** Hay
House Publishers India: www.hayhouse.co.in

*Editorial supervision:* Jill Kramer

**Library of Congress Control Number:** 2009936346

**ISBN:** 978-1-4019-2744-8
**Digital ISBN:** 978-1-4019-2865-0

26  25  24  23  22  21  20  19  18  17
1st edition, July 1999

Printed in the United States of America

This product uses responsibly sourced papers and/or recycled
materials. For more information, see www.hayhouse.com.

# CONTENTS

# Contents

# COLORS & NUMBERS AT A GLANCE

| NUMBER | COLOR(S) | GEM(S)/ PRECIOUS METAL(S) | KEY WORD |
|--------|----------|---------------------------|----------|
| 1 | red | ruby | beginnings |
| 2 | orange | moonstone | cooperate |
| 3 | yellow | topaz | enjoyment |
| 4 | green | emerald/jade | practical |
| 5 | blue | turquoise/ aquamarine | change |
| 6 | indigo (navy blue) | pearl/sapphire/ lapis | responsibility |
| 7 | purple/violet | amethyst | faith |
| 8 | beige/brown/ pink | diamond | achievement |
| 9 | all pastels | opals/gold | completion |
| 11/2 | black/white or pearl gray | silver | intuition |
| 22/4 | coral/russet | coral/copper | greatnesss |

# COLORS & NUMBERS

The study of color is fascinating. We are surrounded by color at all times. Even the so-called colorless has color. A world without color is hard to imagine.

When we think of color, nature may first come to mind. We look forward to the first soft green that confirms that spring is on its way. To see crocuses and daffodils burst out of the thawing ground warms our hearts. The developing of the full lush green and colors of midsummer enables us to feel the abundance of the earth. Then comes the breathtaking autumn spectacle of the yellows, oranges, and reds. When they are gone, winter moves in with its quiet white blanket of snow, and the gray trunks and branches of the trees. We await spring once more.

How many times have we watched a sunset or a sunrise and marveled at the incredible colors? Sunrise on the desert is an awe-filled experience. From early dawn to midday to dusk to midnight, there are thousands of gradations of light and color. When we take the time to look up to the blue of the sky, we feel the tranquility and peace of the open expanse of space. Colors no longer merely serve as a decorative or ornamental function. They affect us in deeper ways.

Color is an essential part of our lives. Yet most of us remain largely ignorant of the benefit to be gained from our conscious use of color. Each color vibrates with its own energy, which we can use to enhance our lives.

The study of numbers is ancient and respected. Pythagoras, the Greek philosopher, who is often considered to be the father of numerology, felt "numbers to be the ultimate elements of the universe." Even as late as the Renaissance, churches were constructed using mystical number systems that the architects believed enhanced an experience of God while within their walls.

Colors and numbers both have significance. In this book they are used together, as numerology teaches us that each number has an associated color; and that each month, each day, the vibrations change. As the number vibrations change, so do the colors.

There are so many ways in which we can cooperate with Life. Consciously using our personal numbers and colors is one way for our days to flow smoother. This book shows us yet another way to integrate colors and numbers into our daily living practices and bring them into balance. Numbers and colors fill our days, and they are useful to our lives and attitudes. They may form a basis for our affirmations and our declarations of ourselves, which is exactly the purpose of this book.

Everything seems to be numbered. Streets and houses and telephones and bank accounts are all numbered. Every appliance and electrical gadget is numbered. So are holidays and calendars and Social Security cards and credit cards and paper money. But the most personal numbers we have are our own ages and our birthday numbers.

Color is also everywhere in our lives. We all eat food, we wear clothing, and many of us wear jewels and gemstones. We color our rooms and our furniture. Our mode of transportation is colored, as is our place of business. When we consciously choose colors and gems and food and clothing that blend with our own personal vibratory rates on a daily basis, we enhance our ability to flow with the currents of life. A healthy attitude toward ourselves and our lives is often reflected in the colors we wear.

Men and women, young and elderly, active and sedentary—all of you will find meaning by assimilating colors and numbers into your lives. Whatever your lifestyle may be, no matter where you may live, the use of color in your life is constant—and numbers are everywhere.

All colors are good, and we feel more comfortable with certain colors at certain times. Our day-to-day living can be enhanced by surrounding ourselves with the colors that are most harmonious with our own personal vibrations for that day. It is the study of numbers that reveals our daily, monthly, and yearly vibrations. When we choose the color that is associated with those particular vibrations and pay attention to what that number is telling us, we are more in tune with Life.

As you will see, each PERSONAL DAY has a color that vibrates with the number of that day. Each PERSONAL DAY also has a jewel that resonates to the color and number. Gems, like colors, have vibrations that, if worn, can enhance a desired mood. There is also a key phrase that sets the tone for this PERSONAL DAY.

I have added an affirmation for each PERSONAL DAY, and I encourage you to concentrate on these positive ideas. I like saying them in the morning shortly after I wake up, preparing for a fresh, new, fun-filled day with plenty of learning and growth.

We each have our own personal number vibrations and personal color vibrations. Some of these numbers, like our birth dates, are permanent. We also have temporary personal colors that change with the calendar. By consciously surrounding ourselves with our personal colors, we become more in tune with the cosmic forces.

In this book, let us explore one aspect of the study of numbers as applied to the use of color in our daily lives.

In the next section, I explain the methods used to find your own PERSONAL YEAR vibration, your PERSONAL MONTH vibration, and your PERSONAL DAY vibration.

● ● ●   ● ● ●

# CALCULATING YOUR PERSONAL YEAR, MONTH, AND DAY

First, there is a Universal Year (the current year) vibration. This vibration is in operation for everyone. We find the number that corresponds with it by adding the four digits of the current year. For instance, the year 2010 is figured by adding $2 + 0 + 1 + 0 = 3$. This tells us that 2010 is a #3 Universal Year.

In numerology, we continue reducing numbers until we have a single digit. Therefore, if the year were 2029, we would add $2 + 0 + 2 + 9 = 13$. And then we would continue reducing the numbers: $1 + 3 = 4$. This would show us that 2029 is a #4 Universal Year.

## *Personal Year*

To discover your PERSONAL YEAR VIBRA-TION, add your own BIRTH MONTH AND BIRTH DAY to the current UNIVERSAL YEAR.

If your birthday is October 23, you add:

10 (for October)
23 (for the day)
 3 (for the Universal Year, 2010)
36  3 + 6 = 9

2010 = #9 PERSONAL YEAR

## *Personal Month*

To find your PERSONAL MONTH VIBRA-
TION for the current month, add your PER-
SONAL YEAR to the calendar month. Using the
previous example, if your PERSONAL YEAR is a
#9 and it is currently the month of March, you
would calculate as follows: #9 (Personal Year)
+ 3 (March) = 12. (Remember, reduce double-
digit numbers to a single digit.) Your PERSON-
AL MONTH VIBRATION would be #3.

 9 (for Personal Year as above)
 3 (for Calendar Month, March)
12  1 + 2 = 3

March 2010 = #3 Personal Month

## *Personal Day*

To find your PERSONAL DAY VIBRATION, add your PERSONAL MONTH to the calendar day.

Using the previous example of March 2010, if this were a #3 PERSONAL MONTH for you, and today is March 1, add the PERSONAL MONTH number to the calendar day:

For March 1, 2010, add:

3  (for Personal Month)
<u>1</u>  (for Calendar Day, March 1)
4

March 1, 2010 = #4 PERSONAL DAY

Once you have determined your Personal Day, then each day follows in numerical sequence, from #1 to #9. So after a #9 Personal Day, you will move to a #1 Personal Day. This same procedure will follow for the remainder of the month. When you enter a new Personal Month, you begin your calculations again.

Blank calendar pages are provided in this book so you may calculate your own personal numbers. It is much easier to do them all at once so your numbers are ready for you as you need them. You may place this book near your closet or bathroom so you can easily refer to it each morning before dressing.

If your calculations for your Personal vibrations total an 11 or 22, do not reduce these numbers to a 2 or 4. The numbers 11 and 22 are considered Master Numbers. They indicate that you are being given an opportunity to operate for that period on a higher vibration. You are more in tune at this time with higher, more universal principles operating in your world and in the world as a whole. Write them as "11/2" or "22/4" so that you are reminded that you have a choice of being the 2 or reaching up to the 11, or a 4 reaching for 22. For instance, the 2 follows a leader; the 11 *is* the leader. The 4 works for the self; the 22 works for the community.

A good thing to know is that whatever the Personal Year, the first Personal Month will be the next number. For instance, January of a #8 Personal Year will be a #9 Personal Month. The 1st day of a #9 Personal Month will be a #1 Personal Day.

### Double and Triple Intensity Days

The Personal Day numbers of the 9th, 18th, and 27th of each calendar month will be the same numbers as the number of the Personal Month. For example, in a #6 Personal Month, the 9th, 18th, and 27th will all be #6 Personal Days. These are DOUBLE INTENSITY Days, which you may wish to star in your calendar. On Double Intensity days, the energy surrounding the specific indications will be intensified doubly, meaning that you have an even greater opportunity to utilize these energies for your benefit and growth.

September is always a special month. The number of the month of September is always the same number as that of your Personal Year. Therefore, the 9th, 18th, and 27th days of September are always TRIPLE INTENSITY. For instance, in a #6 Personal Year, September will be a #6 Personal Month for you; therefore, the entire month will be intensified. In September, the 9th, 18th, and 27th will also be #6 Personal Days of TRIPLE INTENSITY. You may star these days in your calendar as well, perhaps with a different-colored pen, to indicate that the energies will be tripled on these days.

## Helpful Hints

The last two months of a calendar year are always the same Personal Month numbers as the beginning two months of the next calendar year. However, the yearly personal vibrations will be different. In a #6 Personal Year, November will be a #8 Personal Month, and December will be a #9 Personal Month. In the following two months of the next calendar year (which will be your #7 Personal Year), January will be a #8 Personal Month, and February will be a #9 Personal Month. The numbers will be the same, but the yearly personal vibrations will be different, as you will now be in a #7 Personal Year.

Of course, you can do anything on any day; however, if you take advantage of the specific energy that this day presents, you will feel more in harmony with life. If it is snowing, it is not in your best interest to go out in shorts and bare feet. Your day would be more comfortable if you wore clothing that was appropriate for snow. And so it is with life. There are times when certain behaviors and activities are more appropriate and comfortable than others. Some days it just feels RIGHT to go shopping or do your banking—or it may feel RIGHT to scrub your floors. You are keying into the energies that surround you and your life at all times. This book presents a way to specifically tap into them.

In numerology, black is seldom used. On a 11/2 day, black may be worn if it is combined with white, although I always feel pearl gray and silver are more nourishing colors to wear on those days. Black is the absence of color, and in many years of counseling, I found that people who wore a lot of black, or who wore black all the time, were seldom happy people. Black has a tendency to confine and repress the spirit. If you have an emotional problem and/or wear black frequently, I would suggest that you stay away from it for a month and see if you do not become more cheerful. You may even find that you're having a lot more fun!

If you're using these ideas for the first time, it may take you a while to develop a wardrobe that incorporates all the colors in clothing for each season. In the meantime, use whatever you have on hand. It doesn't have to be a whole outfit. A scarf or a belt or a handkerchief—or even colorful underwear—will do nicely. Sometimes it's just carrying a colored pen or even putting a few flowers in a vase to remind you of the color vibration for the day. Give a loved one or friend a gift in his or her own Personal Day color.

The food we eat is also colorful. Therefore, the colors we take into our bodies in the form of food are as meaningful as the colors we wear and with which we surround ourselves. For instance, on a red #1 Personal Day, red apples, tomatoes, or beets might attract and nourish us. (Refer to the food-color chart starting on page 57 for other ideas.)

As you enter a new Personal Year, you could buy something for your home that will reflect this color all year long. You might purchase a new bedspread, or paint your favorite room a pleasing shade of your Personal Year color. Perhaps you might buy yourself a ring or a pendant. If you are ready to buy a new car, your Personal Year vibration could influence the color you choose. Use your imagination to bring meaningful color into your life. Your imagination is reflective of your image of yourself and the love you are developing for yourself.

When in doubt—if you don't have the appropriate color at hand for your Personal Day—you can always use the color for your Personal Month or Personal Year. The number and color of your Personal Year is like background music for everything you will do that year.

*Try it, it's fun! See what happens.*

## *Using Your Numbers*

Now that you have calculated your own current Personal Year, Month, and Day, turn to the section that explains your Personal Year. Read the indications for your Personal Year and what this year means for you. The Personal Year is the background music for your Personal Day. Each day when you arise, turn to the number section that corresponds to the number for your Personal Day. Then, meditate on the concepts and affirmations I have presented that will help you achieve the most good from your Personal Day.

The indications for the Personal Day are to be used in conjunction with the Personal Month and Personal Year. The indications for the Personal Month are the same as the Personal Year of the same number, so you will turn to the section on Personal Year to find the indications for your Personal Month. I prefer to concentrate on TODAY, and therefore utilize the indications for the Personal Day and Personal Year more than for the Personal Month.

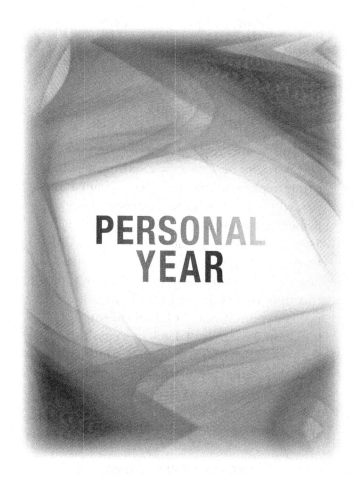

PERSONAL
YEAR

# #1 PERSONAL YEAR

| Color | Gem |
|-------|-----|
| RED | RUBY |

### Key Word
BEGINNINGS

This is the year for new beginnings, for new starts, for new ideas, for anything new. It is a time to plant, to sow seeds. Seeds planted this year will have an effect on the next eight years. Remember, seeds do not come up overnight. They must first germinate and take root. Only then do they grow. Give your ideas a chance to take root. Develop a plan for what you want in this nine-year cycle, and begin to work on it now. Be yourself, and push forward with determination. Take control. Look to yourself rather than to partnerships or unions. During this time period, independence and self-promotion have a strong influence. Lay your groundwork now. Stay busy and keep things moving. This is your year to pioneer and break new ground.

**"I BREAK NEW GROUND
AND BEGIN NEW VENTURES!"**

# #2 PERSONAL YEAR

**Color**
ORANGE

**Gem**
MOONSTONE

## Key Word
COOPERATE

The seeds you planted last year are under the ground ready to germinate. This year you deserve some rest and quiet. Make sure that you have it. Study and acquire knowledge. Practice diplomacy and tact. Sharing and teamwork are best. Be very cooperative. Do not force anything this year. Be patient and wait. That which is right for you will come to you. Pay attention to details. Collect what you need. Look behind the scenes. Opportunities are on the way. Think, plan, and be peaceful. Stay calm. Love is favored. This is a very good year for relationships and partnerships.

**"I TRUST THE PROCESS OF LIFE
TO UNFOLD IN DIVINE RIGHT ORDER!"**

# #3 PERSONAL YEAR

| **Color** | **Gem** |
|-----------|---------|
| YELLOW | TOPAZ |

## Key Word
ENJOYMENT

This is your year for fun. That which you started two years ago is now beginning to come to life. Believe in yourself. The seeds are beginning to send out roots. The birth is evident. All is well, and you feel it. Love is everywhere. It's a time for friends and doing things you enjoy. Entertain, and go to parties and gatherings. Take vacations and holidays. The influence this year is social and artistic. Express yourself creatively as much as possible. Laugh and smile and sing and dance and spread sunshine all around you. Your year will be full of joy.

**"I LOVE LIFE AND THE JOY OF LIVING!"**

# #4 PERSONAL YEAR

### Color
GREEN

### Gems
EMERALD/JADE

### Key Word
PRACTICAL

Now it's time to get back to work. The seeds are sending shoots up through the ground. Do your weeding. Be productive and organized. Build your foundation. Be busy and follow your schedule. Take inventory. Get your life in order and attend to the details. Use self-discipline and avoid being lazy. Do things cheerfully, and you will have all the energy you need. Take good care of your health. You are building for the future, so be constructive. Solve problems this year. The more effort you give, the more rewards you will reap. Everything will turn out well.

**"I TURN EVERYTHING INTO
AN OPPORTUNITY!"**

# #5 PERSONAL YEAR

| Color | Gems |
|-------|------|
| BLUE | TURQUOISE/ AQUAMARINE |

**Key Word**
CHANGE

Freedom and change are in the air. After all your work last year, you deserve a vacation. Let this be your year to dress up. Put your best foot forward. Drop the routine. Discard old ideas. Do something unusual. Be different. Get out and experience life in a new way. It's a great year to learn a new language or experience life in a new place. Make changes—in yourself, your home, your lifestyle, your business. Make sure these changes benefit others, too. See as many people as you can. Look for good surprises. Yet don't throw all caution to the wind. Be active, not restless. This can be a very satisfying year.

**"I WELCOME CHANGE AND EXPAND MY BOUNDARIES!"**

# #6 PERSONAL YEAR

### Color
INDIGO (navy blue)

### Gems
PEARL/SAPPHIRE/LAPIS

### Key Word
RESPONSIBILITY

Now it's time for home, family, community, and friends. The plants are flowering. Make your home the center of your life. Be responsible, fair, and just. Be of service, and accept your duties willingly. Take care of all your personal belongings, people, places, and things. This year is the best of all for marriage. It's the perfect year to move into a new home. Make music a big part of your life. Do all your entertaining at home. Set your standards and keep them. Complete whatever you start. Maintain rhythm and harmony in your life. Anything you do for the benefit of the group is good. Be the counselor. Give assistance whenever it is needed. This is a deeply satisfying year.

**"I ACCEPT MY RESPONSIBILITIES
WITH LOVE AND JOY!"**

# #7 PERSONAL YEAR

### Colors
PURPLE/VIOLET

### Gem
AMETHYST

## Key Word
FAITH

This is an inner year. The fruit is just beginning to grow on the vine, and you must have faith that it will ripen. Take time for reflection, study, and self-analysis. Spend lots of time alone, and use it constructively. Analyze your thoughts and actions. What would you like to change about yourself? The number 7 always reveals things that one normally does not see. Look over your life. This year is for inner growth and preparation. Don't reach out or try to force things; let things come to you. Release the business world as much as possible. Meditate; be introspective. Leave your social life for another time. You may travel to learn more about yourself. This is a spiritual year, so flow with it. Allow your soul to grow.

**"I ENJOY THE INNER QUEST
AND FIND MANY ANSWERS!"**

# #8 PERSONAL YEAR

| **Colors** | **Gem** |
|---|---|
| BEIGE/BROWN/PINK | DIAMOND |

## Key Word
ACHIEVEMENT

This is the success year. It's harvest time. That which you began eight years ago is now ready. Take your product to the market. Business and all material things are yours now. Put out some effort and you will accomplish a lot. Go after what you want. Be the executive, the manager, the organizer. Be efficient and businesslike. Be self-confident. Be honest and fair in all your dealings. You can accomplish big things. Look for unexpected sources of money. Business trips are favored. This is your year to achieve. Go for it!

**"I AM THE PROSPEROUS, SUCCESSFUL EXECUTIVE OF MY WORLD!"**

# #9 PERSONAL YEAR

### Colors
ALL PASTELS

### Gem/Precious Metal
OPALS/GOLD

### Key Word
COMPLETION

It's a time for completion and fulfillment. The garden is finished for this cycle, yet some of the crops continue to produce. This is the year of spring-cleaning. Get into the corners. Review everything and toss out all that is no longer useful in your life—people, places, ideas, and things. If it's finished, let it go. Don't hang on. Many things will pass out of your life this year. Bless them and release them. You are making room for next year. There is much happiness around you. This is a year for endings. Do not begin new things. Don't look for new love affairs now; they won't last. Enjoy the artistic part of life. Take a long trip and learn about, and give to, others. Be tolerant, compassionate, and forgiving. Love must be shared with all. Really understand the kinship of everyone on this planet. The old cycle closes. Make ready for the new one next year.

**"I AM SATISFIED, FULFILLED,
AND COMPLETE!"**

# #11/2 PERSONAL YEAR

**Colors**
BLACK/WHITE
or PEARL GRAY

**Precious Metal**
SILVER

**Key Word**
INTUITION

11/2 is a Master Number. Rise above daily routines. Shine like a star. Set new standards for yourself on the internal level. Do more investigating on the spiritual and metaphysical side of life. Universal love is more important than personal love this year. Keep your own inner peace, no matter what. New Thought topics will have more interest for you. This is not a business year, although you will have lots of good ideas for later. Live up to your ideals. Prepare yourself. Fame and honor could come to you this year. Now is a time for inner growth, illumination, and reflection.

**"I LISTEN TO THE INNER
VOICE OF WISDOM!"**

# #22/4 PERSONAL YEAR

| Colors | Gem/Precious Metal |
|---|---|
| CORAL/RUSSET | CORAL/COPPER |

## Key Word
### GREATNESS

22/4 is a Master Number. Superior accomplishments can be achieved if you rise above the 4. The community needs you. If you work only for yourself, you will miss the full advantage of the year. If you work on big plans for the good of many, then your projects will be successful. This is an opportunity for a power year involving big projects. Build something worthwhile. Use all your mental powers. You don't get a year like this often. Prominence and power can be yours.

**"I WORK FOR THE GOOD OF THE
PLANET, AND I AM BLESSED!"**

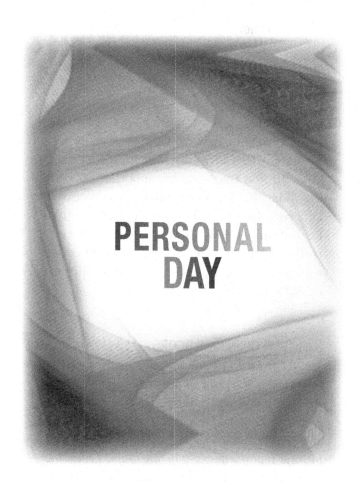

PERSONAL
DAY

# #1 PERSONAL DAY

**Color**
RED

**Gem**
RUBY

## TIME TO BEGIN

Be independent. Do what you want to do. Go after things. Go to new places. Meet new people. Try out new ideas. Begin a new job. Be active. This is a great day for a first date. You will find that men are important in your life today. Be the leader today. Trust yourself and your intuition. Be original and creative. Be ambitious. Feel your own power. Be courageous. Anger, stubbornness, impatience, or worry may tend to undermine your abilities. Look for the new.

### "I OPEN NEW DOORS TO LIFE!"

*Today I trust the Infinite Wisdom within me to lead me and guide me in new areas of living. I am safe and secure as I step out, trusting the Process of Life to be there for me. Life supports me every step of the way. I am fed, clothed, housed, and loved in ways that are deeply fulfilling to me. I meet the new with open arms, aware that it will soon become familiar. Knowing that all friends and lovers were once strangers to me, I welcome new people into my life. Today is a glorious day for me.*

# #2 PERSONAL DAY

| **Color** | **Gem** |
|-----------|---------|
| ORANGE | MOONSTONE |

## COOPERATE

Be peaceful. This is a time to agree with others. Do more than your share. Be patient, tolerant, and diplomatic. It's time to be receptive. Collect that which you need. Look for that special antique. Observe, listen, and think. Put others at ease, and be aware of their feelings. Create harmony. Enjoy your female friends. Relax; be gentle and pleasant. Wait.

### "I AM KIND, AND CONSIDERATE OF OTHERS!"

*Yesterday I planted in the Garden of Life. Today I patiently wait for the seeds to awaken. I have time and consideration for everyone around me. I joyfully help wherever I can, easing the load of others. That which I give out returns to me multiplied. I gather to myself that which I need for the future. This is a harmonious, receptive, loving, peaceful day.*

# #3 PERSONAL DAY

| Color | Gem |
|-------|-----|
| YELLOW | TOPAZ |

## IT'S PARTY TIME

Laugh and have fun. All people are important. It's a social day. Sing, dance, and play. Express yourself. Love everybody. Today truly embodies the joy of living. Look beautiful. Feel handsome. Experience the joy that is in you, and radiate it all around you. Bless everyone and everything. Make others smile. Let your creativity express itself freely. This is the best day for shopping. It's a people day. Love everyone you come into contact with.

## "I RADIATE JOY AND SHARE IT WITH OTHERS!"

*Joy flows through my veins and is expressed in every part of my being. I know my seeds are sprouting, and it is a time for rejoicing. I am joyously exuberant and in harmony with all of life. My life is a party to be experienced and shared with everyone I know. My creativity flows, and I give of it freely. I am beautiful, and everybody loves me. All is well in my world, and I share this feeling with others.*

# #4 PERSONAL DAY

| Color | Gems |
|-------|------|
| GREEN | EMERALD/JADE |

## TIME TO WORK

It's time to get up early. Get those chores done. You have lots of energy today. Get going on those projects. Pay your bills. Write those letters. Balance the budget. Clean the house. Wash the car. Be organized and dependable. Do your repairs. The work you do today is lasting. Have a health checkup. Get things ready for tomorrow.

## "I AM ORGANIZED AND PRODUCTIVE!"

*The first tender shoots are coming through the ground, and there is work to do. I joyfully pull the weeds of negativity from within my consciousness. The Power of the Universe backs me in this endeavor, and I have boundless energy. I get things done easily and quickly. I build firm foundations for tomorrow. I am healthy in body, mind, and spirit.*

# #5 PERSONAL DAY

| **Color** | **Gems** |
|-----------|----------|
| BLUE | TURQUOISE/ AQUAMARINE |

## CHANGE AND SURPRISE

Look your best. Really dress up. Get out and look for the new. Positive change is in the air. Today you are free. Expect a surprise. Do something different. Be flexible. Change your routine. Promote and advertise yourself or your products. Look at another side of life. Give something away. Sell something. This is the best day for haircuts or surgery. You feel free today.

### "I WELCOME CHANGE AND REJOICE IN THE NEW!"

*The crop is growing well and takes care of itself, soaking in the sunshine of life and the nourishment of the soil. I am free to allow the different experiences of life to come in. I am alert to a wonderful, positive surprise that benefits me in a delightful way. I look and feel terrific. Here I am, world, open and receptive to all good, which I accept with joy, pleasure, and gratitude.*

# #6 PERSONAL DAY

| **Color** | **Gems** |
| --- | --- |
| INDIGO (navy blue) | PEARL/SAPPHIRE/ LAPIS |

## ADJUSTMENT TIME

Take a personal inventory. Look at your home. Could you make it more comfortable? How about you? Could you be more polished? Review your diet. Does it need adjusting? Look at your personality. Could it be more cheerful? Look at your responsibilities. Do any need taking care of? Are you sticking your nose into other people's business? If so, let go. Do you owe anything? Now is the time to pay up. Enjoy your family. Entertain at home. Fill your day with music. If possible, do not travel. Save creative writing for another day. Teachers excel, and group work is favored. This is a wonderful day for moving into a new home.

### "MY HOME IS A PEACEFUL HAVEN!"

*My plants are in bloom and are a joy to behold. They enhance my home, and I tend to them carefully. Where needed, I easily make adjustments to my home. It is a comfortable place to be—for me and others. I open my home and welcome guests with music and love. They are like a loving family to me.*

# #7 PERSONAL DAY

| **Colors** | **Gem** |
|---|---|
| PURPLE/VIOLET | AMETHYST |

## LOOK WITHIN

Be alone, at least for part of the day. Be still. Read. Think. Listen to your inner soul. Drop the business world. If you pursue money today, it will run from you. If you keep still and wait, things will come to you. Study something spiritual or scientific. If you read the scriptures, choose Matthew 6 on this day. Work with your plants. Take a long walk or a drive in the country. The number 7 always reveals something. Meditate. Be open.

## "I LOOK WITHIN AND RECEIVE ANSWERS!"

*I have faith that the Universe is in the process of producing enormous good for me. So silently I take time to go within, to be in touch with my own inner wisdom. I look with love at nature and all her beauty, and I am renewed and refreshed. I trust Life to take care of me. I know that whatever I need will always be there for me. The Power that supplies my breath will supply all else just as easily and freely.*

# #8 PERSONAL DAY

| **Colors** | **Gem** |
| --- | --- |
| BEIGE/BROWN/PINK | DIAMOND |

## SUCCESSFUL BUSINESS

Ambition stirs within you. It's a time for advancement. Look and act successful. It's a good business day. Be an executive. Organize and reorganize. Use your best judgment. Pay your bills. Do all your financial and legal work. It's the ideal day for signing leases or contracts. Go to the gym or have a health checkup. You might receive unexpected money. Help someone less fortunate. Success is already yours.

## "I AM POWERFUL AND PROSPEROUS!"

*The bountiful harvest is in and ready for the marketplace. I am the executive of my life and affairs. I have innate good judgment, for I am connected at all times to Universal Intelligence. With the Universe as my partner, I go from success to success. I am the benevolent and loving director of the kingdom I have created. The more I help others, the more I prosper and grow. Where I am, everybody wins.*

# #9 PERSONAL DAY

| Colors | Gems/Precious Metal |
|--------|---------------------|
| ALL PASTELS | OPALS/GOLD |

## HUMANITY

All the world is your family. Be a humanitarian. Help everyone you can. Be generous and kind. No beginnings today; just finish things up. It's not a good day for a first date—it won't last. No shopping unless it's for a gift. Clean out closets and drawers. If you don't use something you own, give it away or sell it. Release all that no longer benefits you—things, ideas, habits, relationships. Be an artist. Use your creative talents. It's a great day for a public performance. What you give out will come back to you, so give only the best. Close the chapter; tomorrow you start anew.

### "I AM ONE WITH ALL OF LIFE. THE WHOLE WORLD IS MY FAMILY!"

*The work is done, the cycle is complete. Everything is clean. I release and let go; I gladly give away all that I no longer need. I am generous with my fellow travelers on this planet, for they are my brothers and sisters. I forgive and forget. I give freely of my heart and possessions. I have understanding, fulfillment is mine, and I am deeply satisfied. All is well in my world.*

# #11/2 PERSONAL DAY

| Colors | Precious Metal |
|---|---|
| BLACK/WHITE | SILVER |
| or PEARL GRAY | |

## FOLLOW YOUR STAR

11/2 is a Master Number. Leave commercialism behind you. The vibrations today are highly attuned and very spiritual. Your intuition is strong. Do not force anything. Be silent. Keep the peace. Let the day flow and be on time. Do not read. Go within. Don't argue; you won't win. It's not your fault anyway. Be a shining light in the world. You can be greatly inspired today, or you can inspire others.

## "I FOLLOW MY INNER STAR!"

*I have a direct pipeline of wisdom and knowledge from the highest source. As I turn within, all the answers I seek are there for the asking. Every question I have is easily answered by my own inspiration. I Inspire others. I am a shining example of love and light. Today I sparkle and shine in a quiet and peaceful way.*

# #22/4 PERSONAL DAY

| **Colors** | **Gem/Precious Metal** |
|---|---|
| CORAL/RUSSET | CORAL/COPPER |

## GIVE OF YOURSELF

22/4 is a Master Number. Forget yourself and your own interests. Whatever you do today must be for the universal good. Work for the community or for the world. Any plans you make must be large and for the highest interests of all. Do things for others. It will bring you good fortune.

## "I JOYFULLY BLESS AND PROSPER EVERYONE!"

*It is my joy and pleasure to share all that I have and all that I am with everyone on the planet. I give freely of my talents and abilities and resources. My viewpoint is ever larger, and I work for the highest interests of all concerned. I am one with the Universe now and forevermore.*

# YOUR PERSONAL CALENDAR

**EXAMPLE:** *If* September is your #3 Personal Month, then October will be your #4 Personal Month ...

| | SUN | MON | TUES | WED | THURS | FRI | SAT | |
|---|---|---|---|---|---|---|---|---|
| **2010**<br>S<br>E<br>P<br>T<br>E<br>M<br>B<br>E<br>R | | | | 4 $^1$ | 5 $^2$ | 6 $^3$ | 7 $^4$ | YOUR PERSONAL MONTH **#3** |
| | 8 $^5$ | 9 $^6$ | 1 $^7$ | 11/2* $^8$ | 3 $^9$ | 4 $^{10}$ | 5 $^{11}$ | |
| | 6 $^{12}$ | 7 $^{13}$ | 8 $^{14}$ | 9 $^{15}$ | 1 $^{16}$ | 2 $^{17}$ | *3* $^{18}$ | |
| | 22/4* $^{19}$ | 5 $^{20}$ | 6 $^{21}$ | 7 $^{22}$ | 8 $^{23}$ | 9 $^{24}$ | 1 $^{25}$ | |
| | 11/2* $^{26}$ | 3 $^{27}$ | 4 $^{28}$ | 5 $^{29}$ | 6 $^{30}$ | | | |
| **2010**<br>O<br>C<br>T<br>O<br>B<br>E<br>R | | | | | | 5 $^1$ | 6 $^2$ | YOUR PERSONAL MONTH **#4** |
| | 7 $^3$ | 8 $^4$ | 9 $^5$ | 1 $^6$ | 11/2* $^7$ | 3 $^8$ | *4* $^9$ | |
| | 5 $^{10}$ | 6 $^{11}$ | 7 $^{12}$ | 8 $^{13}$ | 9 $^{14}$ | 1 $^{15}$ | 2 $^{16}$ | |
| | 3 $^{17}$ | 22/4* $^{18}$ | 5 $^{19}$ | 6 $^{20}$ | 7 $^{21}$ | 8 $^{22}$ | 9 $^{23}$ | |
| | 1/8 $^{24/31}$ | 11/2* $^{25}$ | 3 $^{26}$ | *4* $^{27}$ | 5 $^{28}$ | 6 $^{29}$ | 7 $^{30}$ | |

43

# JANUARY

| SUN | MON | TUES | WED | THURS | FRI | SAT |
|-----|-----|------|-----|-------|-----|-----|
|     |     |      |     |       |     |     |
|     |     |      |     |       |     |     |
|     |     |      |     |       |     |     |
|     |     |      |     |       |     |     |
|     |     |      |     |       |     |     |

**YOUR PERSONAL MONTH:**_____

# FEBRUARY

| SUN | MON | TUES | WED | THURS | FRI | SAT |
|-----|-----|------|-----|-------|-----|-----|
|     |     |      |     |       |     |     |
|     |     |      |     |       |     |     |
|     |     |      |     |       |     |     |
|     |     |      |     |       |     |     |
|     |     |      |     |       |     |     |

**YOUR PERSONAL MONTH:**_____

# MARCH

| SUN | MON | TUES | WED | THURS | FRI | SAT |
|-----|-----|------|-----|-------|-----|-----|
|     |     |      |     |       |     |     |
|     |     |      |     |       |     |     |
|     |     |      |     |       |     |     |
|     |     |      |     |       |     |     |
|     |     |      |     |       |     |     |

**YOUR PERSONAL MONTH:** _____

# APRIL

| SUN | MON | TUES | WED | THURS | FRI | SAT |
|-----|-----|------|-----|-------|-----|-----|
|     |     |      |     |       |     |     |
|     |     |      |     |       |     |     |
|     |     |      |     |       |     |     |
|     |     |      |     |       |     |     |
|     |     |      |     |       |     |     |

**YOUR PERSONAL MONTH:**_____

# MAY

| SUN | MON | TUES | WED | THURS | FRI | SAT |
|-----|-----|------|-----|-------|-----|-----|
|     |     |      |     |       |     |     |
|     |     |      |     |       |     |     |
|     |     |      |     |       |     |     |
|     |     |      |     |       |     |     |
|     |     |      |     |       |     |     |

**YOUR PERSONAL MONTH:**_____

# JUNE

| SUN | MON | TUES | WED | THURS | FRI | SAT |
|-----|-----|------|-----|-------|-----|-----|
|     |     |      |     |       |     |     |
|     |     |      |     |       |     |     |
|     |     |      |     |       |     |     |
|     |     |      |     |       |     |     |
|     |     |      |     |       |     |     |

**YOUR PERSONAL MONTH:**_____

# JULY

| SUN | MON | TUES | WED | THURS | FRI | SAT |
|-----|-----|------|-----|-------|-----|-----|
|     |     |      |     |       |     |     |
|     |     |      |     |       |     |     |
|     |     |      |     |       |     |     |
|     |     |      |     |       |     |     |
|     |     |      |     |       |     |     |

**YOUR PERSONAL MONTH:**_____

# AUGUST

| SUN | MON | TUES | WED | THURS | FRI | SAT |
|-----|-----|------|-----|-------|-----|-----|
|     |     |      |     |       |     |     |
|     |     |      |     |       |     |     |
|     |     |      |     |       |     |     |
|     |     |      |     |       |     |     |
|     |     |      |     |       |     |     |

**YOUR PERSONAL MONTH:**_____

# SEPTEMBER

| SUN | MON | TUES | WED | THURS | FRI | SAT |
|-----|-----|------|-----|-------|-----|-----|
|     |     |      |     |       |     |     |
|     |     |      |     |       |     |     |
|     |     |      |     |       |     |     |
|     |     |      |     |       |     |     |
|     |     |      |     |       |     |     |

**YOUR PERSONAL MONTH:**_____

# OCTOBER

| SUN | MON | TUES | WED | THURS | FRI | SAT |
|-----|-----|------|-----|-------|-----|-----|
|     |     |      |     |       |     |     |
|     |     |      |     |       |     |     |
|     |     |      |     |       |     |     |
|     |     |      |     |       |     |     |
|     |     |      |     |       |     |     |

**YOUR PERSONAL MONTH:**_____

# NOVEMBER

| SUN | MON | TUES | WED | THURS | FRI | SAT |
|-----|-----|------|-----|-------|-----|-----|
|     |     |      |     |       |     |     |
|     |     |      |     |       |     |     |
|     |     |      |     |       |     |     |
|     |     |      |     |       |     |     |
|     |     |      |     |       |     |     |

**YOUR PERSONAL MONTH:**_____

# DECEMBER

| SUN | MON | TUES | WED | THURS | FRI | SAT |
|-----|-----|------|-----|-------|-----|-----|
|     |     |      |     |       |     |     |
|     |     |      |     |       |     |     |
|     |     |      |     |       |     |     |
|     |     |      |     |       |     |     |
|     |     |      |     |       |     |     |

**YOUR PERSONAL MONTH:**_____

# COLORS
# IN FOOD

## RED

apples
beets
red cabbage
cherries
radishes
raspberries
strawberries
tomatoes
watermelon
red meats

## ORANGE

apricots
cantaloupe
carrots
mangoes
oranges
persimmons
pumpkins
nectarines
tangerines

## YELLOW

bananas
corn
eggs
grapefruit
lemons
oils
peaches
pineapple
cheese
yams

# GREEN

asparagus
artichokes
avocados
all lettuce
green vegetables
pears

# BLUE

blueberries
loganberries
some grapes
blue plums

# INDIGO (navy blue)

(use the
blue and
violet
foods)

# PURPLE/VIOLET

blackberries
eggplant
dark grapes
purple plums
passion fruit
dulse

# ABOUT
# LOUISE HAY

**Louise Hay** was an inspirational teacher who educated millions since the 1984 publication of her bestseller *You Can Heal Your Life*, which has more than 50 million copies in print worldwide. Renowned for demonstrating the power of affirmations to bring about positive change, Louise was the author of more than 30 books for adults and children, including the bestsellers *The Power Is Within You* and *Heal Your Body*. In addition to her books, Louise produced numerous audio and video programs, card decks, online courses, and other resources for leading a healthy, joyous, and fulfilling life.

Websites: www.louisehay.com, www.healyourlife.com, and www.facebook.com/louiselhay

• • •  • • •

# ALSO BY LOUISE HAY

## BOOKS/KITS

*The Affirmations Coloring Book* (with Alberta Hutchinson)

*All Is Well* (with Mona Lisa Schulz, M.D., Ph.D.)

*The Bone Broth Secret* (with Heather Dane)

*Empowering Women*

*Everyday Positive Thinking*

*Experience Your Good Now!*

*A Garden of Thoughts: My Affirmation Journal*

*Gratitude: A Way of Life* (Louise & Friends)

*Heal Your Body*

*Heal Your Body A–Z*

*Heal Your Mind* (with Mona Lisa Schulz, M.D., Ph.D.)

*Heart Thoughts* (also available in a gift edition)

*I Can Do It*® (book-with-CD)

*Inner Wisdom*

*Letters to Louise*

*Life Loves You* (with Robert Holden)

*Life! Reflections on Your Journey*

*Love Your Body*

*Love Yourself, Heal Your Life Workbook*

*Loving Yourself to Great Health*
(with Ahlea Khadro and Heather Dane)

*Meditations to Heal Your Life*
(also available in a gift edition)

*Mirror Work*

*Modern-Day Miracles* (Louise & Friends)

*The Power Is Within You*

*Power Thoughts*

*Meditations to Heal Your Life* (audio book)
*Morning and Evening Meditations*
*101 Power Thoughts*
*Overcoming Fears*
*The Power Is Within You* (audio book)
*The Power of Your Spoken Word*
*Receiving Prosperity*
*Self-Esteem Affirmations* (subliminal)
*Self-Healing*
*Stress-Free* (subliminal)
*Totality of Possibilities*
*What I Believe and Deep Relaxation*
*You Can Heal Your Life* (audio book)
*You Can Heal Your Life Study Course*
*Your Thoughts Create Your Life*

## DVDs

*Receiving Prosperity*

*You Can Heal Your Life, THE MOVIE*
(also available in an expanded edition)

*You Can Trust Your Life* (with Cheryl Richardson)

## CARD DECKS

*Healthy Body Cards*

*I Can Do It® Cards*

*I Can Do It® Cards . . . for Creativity, Forgiveness,
Health, Job Success, Wealth, Romance*

*Life Loves You Cards* (with Robert Holden)
*Power Thought Cards*
*Power Thoughts for Teens*
*Power Thought Sticky Cards*
*Wisdom Cards*

## CALENDAR

*I Can Do It®️ Calendar* (for each individual year)

and

## THE LOUISE HAY BOOK COLLECTION

(comprising *You Can Heal Your Life, Heal Your Body,* and
*The Power Is Within You* in a single volume)

———————————————

All of the above are available at your local
bookstore, or may be ordered by visiting:

Hay House USA: **www.hayhouse.com®️**
Hay House Australia: **www.hayhouse.com.au**
Hay House UK: **www.hayhouse.co.uk**
Hay House India: **www.hayhouse.co.in**

Louise's Websites: **www.LouiseHay.com®️**
and **www.HealYourLife.com®️**

We hope you enjoyed this Hay House book.
If you'd like to receive our online catalog featuring
additional information on Hay House books and
products, or if you'd like to find out more about the

Hay Foundation, please contact:

Hay House LLC, P.O. Box 5100,
Carlsbad, CA 92018-5100
(760) 431-7695 or (800) 654-5126
(760) 431-6948 (fax) or (800) 650-5115 (fax)
www.hayhouse.com® • www.hayfoundation.org

———

*Published in Australia by:*
Hay House Australia Pty. Ltd.
18/36 Ralph St., Alexandria NSW 2015
*Phone:* 612-9669-4299
*Fax:* 612-9669-4144
www.hayhouse.com.au

*Published in the United Kingdom by:*
Hay House UK, Ltd.
The Sixth Floor, Watson House
54 Baker Street, London W1U 7BU
*Phone:* +44 (0)20 3927 7290
*Fax:* +44 (0)20 3927 7291
www.hayhouse.co.uk


*Published in India by:*
Hay House Publishers India
Muskaan Complex, Plot No. 3, B-2
Vasant Kunj, New Delhi 110 070
*Phone:* 91-11-4176-1620
*Fax:* 91-11-4176-1630
www.hayhouse.co.in

——